The Log

Written by Jill Eggleton
Illustrated by Sandra Cammell

Matt went out
to his pool.
"Look at this," he said.
"A log is in my pool."

Matt got a stick.
He put the stick
under the log.

"Come out, log," he said. "I can't swim with a log in my pool."

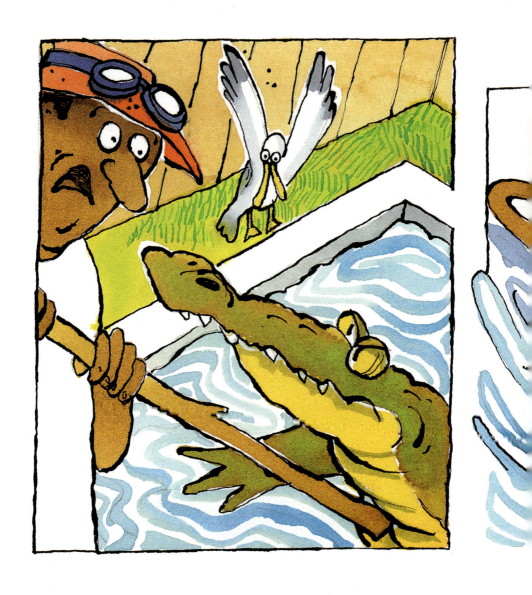

But the log
was a crocodile!

The crocodile went
snap on the stick!
Matt saw its **big** teeth.

"**Help!**" shouted Matt.
"The log is a crocodile!"

Kate came
to the house.
She had some food
and a rope.
She put the food down.

"Come on, Crocodile," she said.
"Get out!"

The crocodile came out.
It went **snap**
on the food.

Kate sat on its tail.
She put the rope
over its mouth.

Kate put the crocodile in the truck.
"You can come with me," she said.
"This pool is **not** for you!"

Speech Bubbles

You can have a swim. The crocodile will not come back.

Thanks! I can't swim with a crocodile.

Guide Notes

Title: The Log
Stage: Early (2) – Yellow

Genre: Fiction
Approach: Guided Reading
Processes: Thinking Critically, Exploring Language, Processing Information
Written and Visual Focus: Speech Bubbles
Word Count: 157

THINKING CRITICALLY
(sample questions)
- What do you think this story could be about?
- Focus on the title and discuss.
- Why do you think the crocodile went into Matt's pool?
- What do you think might have happened if Matt had got into the pool with the crocodile?
- How do you know that Kate knew about crocodiles?
- Where do you think Kate will take the crocodile?

EXPLORING LANGUAGE

Terminology
Title, cover, illustrations, author, illustrator

Vocabulary
Interest words: crocodile, snap, food, rope
High-frequency words: its, some, with
Positional words: out, under, over, in, on, down

Print Conventions
Capital letter for sentence beginnings and names (**M**att, **K**ate), full stops, commas, quotation marks, exclamation marks, question mark